The
KEY
TO
EVERYTHING

By
NORMAN GRUBB

MOODY PRESS
CHICAGO

Reprinted from CHRISTIAN LIFE Magazine. Copyrighted by Sunday Magazine, Inc., 33 S. Wacker Drive, Chicago, Illinois 60606, publishers of CHRISTIAN LIFE.

Large Print Edition, 1975
ISBN: 0-8024-4546-2

Second Printing, 1976

Printed in United States of America

CONTENTS

CHAPTER   PAGE

1. Christ in You   5

2. You Simply Receive   19

3. Your Other Self   36

4. Your New Spirit   56

1
CHRIST IN YOU

When I was in the British army in World War I, God very plainly called me, though I'd planned another career, to join a little independent missionary group just starting in Africa.

I wasn't there very long before I deeply felt my inadequacy.

It wasn't that I was lukewarm for Jesus Christ; it wasn't that I had turned away from Him to some other interest. I was a servant of His, and my whole interest was set on introducing my brother Africans to Him.

The inadequacy I felt in myself first of all was the need of love. I deeply felt, when I got among them, that I just didn't have that love which bridges the gap. With that went the need of faith—and with that the need of power. All of these were linked together.

Response to the Christian message in Central Africa, like the United States, appears to be quite large. But I soon found there was much more profession than possession. I began saying to myself, *Are we bringing the Africans anything really worthwhile? Are we just bringing a code of ethics? Or a liturgy, or historic faith? Have we got something genuinely transforming to transmit to others?*

Then I made the question personal, "Have I?"

As I asked these questions, I discovered that when your ministry is disturbed, it tends also to disturb your personal life. I found myself, as my wife well knew, irritable in a way I hadn't been irritable at home—and critical of others to cover my own failures.

As I doubted, asked questions, and searched the Bible for some kind of an answer to my inadequacies, I found some amazing answers. Some of them have shaken me considerably. They have changed by whole viewpoint—and my experience.

I can't call them revelations, because they are based on *the* revelation, witnessed to by the Spirit—the Bible.

To begin with, my attitude was that God should improve me.

Well, I'm a servant of Jesus Christ, I thought. I've been redeemed by His grace, I belong to Him. I must ask God to make me a better servant of Jesus Christ.

I thought He should channel some love into my heart, some faith, some power, some holiness—and improve me.

I had to learn sharply that self-improvement is both a sin and an impossibility. It came as a considerable shock.

But though my idea of how God should answer my problem was completely wrong, my sense of inadequacy was good. It sent me to the Bible. And my first discovery came as I read one famous verse in the first letter of John: "God is love" (4:16).

Suddenly the *is* stuck out. What dawned on me went something like this: It doesn't say God *has* love, but God *is* love. If somebody *has* a thing, it isn't he himself. It's something just attached to him, as if you've got a coat on or something in your pocket. You just have it, and you can share it. But the Bible doesn't say God *has* love, but God *is* love.

I Could Never Love!

Love, therefore, must not be a thing I can have. Love is exclusively a Person. *God* is love. Therefore, there is no other pure, selfgiving love in the universe beyond Him Himself. Love is exclusively a characteristic of one Person only—and that's not Norman Grubb.

That was a deflation for me. I had thought I could have love imparted to me, channeled into me, and I'd be more loving. But I suddenly found God saying, "You'll never have one iota of love. I am love, and that's the end of it."

Love is a Person; one Person only loving—and that's not I, and that's not you. God is love and, therefore, love is God loving.

That set a new trend of thought going. I began to relate this to my other need of power. And I suddenly found a verse in the first chapter of 1 Corinthians. It says that Christ is the power of God. Not Christ *has* the power, but He *is* the power.

Once again, I had thought power was something which was given to me. It would make me a powerful servant of Jesus Christ. I suddenly found that power, also, is a Person. And that person is not I but is exclusively Christ, who is God; it doesn't matter whether you call Him Father, Son, or Holy Spirit.

Then I came to the one thing every Christian claims to have. Every believing Christian accepts the fact that he has eternal life. He takes it that he has a life which will go on forever in

Heaven: "The gift of God is eternal life through Jesus Christ our Lord" (Romans 6:23).

But I suddenly found that eternal life is not something *I* can ever have—for Jesus did not say, "I *have* the life to give you"—but "I *am* life."

Once again I had found that something I had thought I had—eternal life—is one person only, and that's not I. Jesus Christ is that "eternal life."

But where did I fit into all this?

Finally I came to a statement which gathered all together and finished off my investigations by its absoluteness. The verse was Colossians 3:11, where it says of believers in Christ that "Christ is all and in all."

Christ *is* all, not Christ has all.

And if Christ is all, what's left for me? Not much by my mathematics!

I had thought I was somebody, but then I found that God had taken the lot. Christ is all.

Then I got the link. Christ is all *and in all.*

Then I saw for the first time that the only reason for the existence of the entire creation is to contain the Creator! Not to be something, but to contain Someone.

So there dawned a very important truth. We humans naturally regard the human self as important. But we've got the wrong ideas of the reason of the existence of the self.

An immense distortion has come

into the very warp and woof of humanity. It's the distortion of the ego—of the self. Though we feel self to be important, all of this showed me that self is extremely unimportant.

There is only one Self in the universe who is really important. I would almost say there is only one Self.

Why? Because there's only one Person in the universe who ever said, "I Am."

God said that was His name thousands of years ago when Moses asked what he should say when people would ask, "What is the name of your God?" (Exodus 3:13-14).

We are told that at the end of the history of the universe it is God who will be all in all. God all in all! Then what's left? It's terrific.

Why We Exist

There is only one God, and the human creation is brought into a living relationship with this holy One, so that He can manifest Himself in His perfection of life and love through us.

The whole creation exists because God desired a way in which to manifest Himself. As the Scriptures say, "The whole earth is full of His glory" (Is 6:3). They say that Christ ascended "that he might fill all things" (Ephesians 4:10).

The height is simply this: the rest of creation can contain manifestations of

God; we can contain God as a Person. A person cannot manifest himself as a person through anything else than a person. You can't fellowship with a dog or a stone. You can enjoy the marvels of the atom or of a precious stone, but you can't fellowship with it. But I can fellowship with you because we are of the same makeup.

God can manifest His marvels and His beauty through the flowers and trees. We can view them through the microscope and telescope, and marvel—but we do not say, "That's God."

The greatest marvel, the greatest height of personality, is when we can look at a human being and say, "God is there."

The depth, the dangers, of humanity are that personality means freedom. Intelligent choice is the essence of personality.

Therefore, God appeared to be on the horns of a dilemma when He created people. (Of course, He wasn't, for He knows His own business in the end.) But it appeared so because the people He created could turn around and say, "Thank you very much, I don't want You to live in me."

That's exactly what happened.

We make self our god, not God. We just naturally run our own lives. And that's our whole trouble.

There isn't a single problem in humanity except our self-reactions: not one.

The devil is no trouble. He was dealt with 2,000 years ago.

You neighbor is not your trouble.

Circumstances are not your trouble.

Distorted self, self out of gear, is our problem.

Once we know how to handle the human self and put it back where it belongs, we've found the key to life.

That's what we're going to examine.

2

YOU SIMPLY RECEIVE

Essentially from eternity there has been only one God.

This is difficult to realize. Yet throughout the Word of God it is underlined.

God was before all: He is the beginning and the end, the alpha and the omega.

He is love.

He is inconceivable beauty.

He is the all.

If that is so, then the link between Him and us, whom He has created, is the link between the One and the means of manifesting or making known the One. In other words, our relation to Him is that of containing Him in such a way that He may be recognized.

That is why the primary function of all creation, animate and inanimate, is receptivity. Your basic function, and mine, is the same—simply to receive.

This is demonstrated, silently, around us all the time. It's never better seen than in the springtime.

If there were no receptivity in the trees and flowers and shrubs, we should have a desert around us. These things spring to life because of their quiet reception of the sunlight and moisture poured on them. What they receive they utilize. But utilization is secondary to reception.

In biblical language, we call this *faith.*

Better Seen Than Said

But no finite language can completely portray the infinite. So different illustrations are necessary in order to complete the picture of our relation to Him.

Look at the number of times the Bible calls us vessels. "We have this treasure in earthen vessels, that the excellency of the power may be of God, and not of us" (2 Corinthians 4:7). We are vessels "sanctified, and meet for the master's use, and prepared unto every good work" (2 Timothy 2:21).

Now you see at once the beauty of the illustration: a vessel is a hollow object made to contain something. And God has made us vessels.

Of course, if God makes us vessels, He fills us. God doesn't fool with His creation; if He made anything to be filled, He must see to it that it gets filled.

This is *our* receptivity. The whole function of the vessel is to receive something.

Now get this clear: *the vessel never becomes the liquid, nor the liquid the vessel.* I add this because we humans are so proud that there creeps into us the idea that we can be deified. That is *blasphemy*. There is no such thing as self-deification, except that of Satan, the pseudo-God, and what we share with him. The divine can swell in the human, but forever the human is the human and the divine the divine. God has said, "My glory will I not give to another," (Isaiah 42:8).

That is the vital importance of the vessel illustration: we are forever the container; He is that which we contain. That relationship never changes.

But there are other illustrations which both Jesus and Paul used which give us an enlarged picture of our position as receivers.

The famous one is that used by Jesus when He likened Himself and ourselves to the vine and the branches. Now we get a vital, active relationship. We begin to see that the illustration of the vessel is only part of the truth. A vessel is a dead thing and separate from that which is poured into it. From the vessel you might be led to picture us as simply passive containers. But we're not.

So Jesus gave us the vine and branches illustration. Through this our eyes are opened to the secret of the union—the mystery of the universe: how two can be one and yet remain two.

In this dimension, infinite truth is always in the form of paradox. We never get beyond facts that are seemingly contradictory to common sense.

In this dimension we can never fully comprehend truth through our senses. Our reason cannot teach it to us. We have to live with opposites which don't meet, with facts that are, to our understanding, not completely logical. It is good for us to recognize this, and to learn to accept both sides—both ways of knowing—in their proper proportions.

This illustration of the vine and the branches is one of those paradoxes.

The living God, the living Christ, and I actually become one person and function as one person. Separation is impossible. It has disappeared. We function entirely and forever and naturally as one person. And yet we remain two!

The Mystery We Live In

Two in one; one in two. We see the paradox in the vine and the branch illustration because, though the vine and the branch make one, Jesus says that the branch must "abide in the vine" (John 15:4). Though the vine is the life and the branch the channel, yet the branch does things. It utilizes the sap and produces leaf and flower and fruit.

But its activity is secondary to its receptivity. This is where we fail. We make activity a substitute for receptivity. It is its outcome.

Paul gave us another illustration: that of head and body. Head and body make one organism, one life.

You can't divide head and body. My name is Norman Grubb. But my head is not Norman and my body Grubb! You can't divide the two.

Paul tells us the same thing. For instance, 1 Corinthians 12:12 speaks of the body of Christ as *being* Christ. It says, "As the body [the body is, of course, the believers joined to Christ] is one and hath many members, so also is Christ."

We are part of a vital organism which is an ascended, glorious, perfect Christ—the eternal Christ.

We are part of Him, yet we remain, ourselves.

Self-Confidence Is Not Security

In that relationship we are all dependent. Exactly as the body is dependent on the head and the head governs the body, so we forever remain the dependent member in the union.

And the union is never safe until we know that.

So, until you have a few good knocks on the head and discover your conceited self, you're not safe to know the union. Maybe you've had plenty of knocks. They're the healthiest things we can have. We've got to be made safe and understanding for this tremendous relationship.

He is the Lord. We are the cooperators. We are receivers.

Basically every one of us has regarded life as something *we* must live, although we are glad to have the help and grace of God to assist us. Even though we are redeemed people, without realizing our error, we rely mainly on our self-activity.

Basically, every one of us has thought, "We're the people, let's get on with the work."

That is the reason for the long periods of training through which we read God took all His servants in Bible times. Look at Moses. Few can equal his consecration. He threw away a throne as "the son of Pharaoh's daughter," with all "the treasures of Egypt" and "pleasures of sin for a season." And he did all this for the mysterious Christ who had not even come—for he "esteemed the reproach of Christ greater riches," the record says (Hebrews 11:23-26).

Yet there was one thing that Moses had not renounced. That was Moses.

"Learned in all the wisdom of the Egyptians," highly trained, highly educated, "mighty in words and in deeds" (Acts 7:22), he thought the enslaved Israelites would understand that he was their obvious deliverer; and he set out to deliver them. Angered by an Egyptian maltreating one of his people, he beat and killed him.

But Pharoah sent the police after him—and what did Moses do? All he had left was a good pair of legs. So he ran.

A healthy body is useful—but you

need more than two good legs to carry you through life for God! Moses had thought he could do the job; now he found he couldn't. He couldn't find God because, until he had come to an end of himself, God was a distant Person to him.

Unless you have come to the bottom of self you don't know basically in a crisis just how to find God. You can't find God when He's found you. He's just there. The Spirit must teach you. You just say, "That's fine, Lord, carry on." You are thoroughly natural.

I believe in being thoroughly unvarnished with God! That's putting it in extreme form, but what I mean is that a great deal of our pious talk and reverent attitudes and language is a cloak for insincerity. Men of God, God's familiars, God's friends, talk back and forth with Him in plain language.

But Moses, like every one of us, had to learn that you don't do God's work by self-effort and self-wisdom.

Unquenchable Energy

Forty years later, Moses saw what he had not been ready to see before. He saw a queer object where he was tending sheep in the wilderness. It was a common bush on fire. Bur the curious thing, as he watched it, was that it didn't go out.

That is where God showed Moses what humanity is meant to be: a common bush aflame with God.

But a man must be common first. Moses, in his own opinion, had been a very uncommon royal bush, and God doesn't live in uncommon royal bushes. Then Moses saw this sight: God's presence, God's word out of a common bush—and as the divine fire consumes the bush, it refuels it: "that bush was not consumed" (Exodus 3:2).

That's exactly what God does. The divine life keeps flowing in, as you give it out.

That is receptivity: the key to true humanity. *Then* you move out into activity.

No one is active like a Christian, because he is motivated by the divine resources, the divine power, the divine Person. We've got to learn by our hard knocks to clear out of the way and recognize Another functioning; get His voice, His plans, His resources. Then we come back into the situation as servant, not boss.

Once you have come to understand that your basic function is a constant recognition of Another, the whole of life is transformed.

It isn't a matter of continually allowing Him to come into your life, because you have received Him. But it is the recognition of Another.

Another is the functioning one.

Another is the Person who inspires the prayers and imparts the faith and thinks the thoughts through our minds and expresses His compassion through our hearts and puts our bodies into action.

Once you've seen that, you see that He is the illimitable One.

Then you relax and say, "This is what life is basically: Another living His life in me."

You've got your key to everything.

Every problem becomes an opportunity.

Every tough spot becomes a chance to enjoy the luxury of seeing Him deliver us out of it.

And you welcome such spots.

3

YOUR OTHER SELF

Normal humanity is God-indwelt. Humanity which is not indwelt by Deity is subhuman.

Can you offer proof of that, you say? Yes, I can. I can give you proof from the only perfect human who has ever lived on earth.

Jesus Christ was a real human. (That's why I love to call Him Jesus, though He is the Lord Jesus Christ.) He was the Son of God, but if He called Himself the Son of God five times, He called Himself Son of man fifty-five times. Which means He was a representative man—one of us.

Notice what Jesus said each time He was challenged on the source of His power to work miracles or authority to say what He did. Every time He answered, "The Son can do nothing of Himself."

In other words, His basic self-consciousness as a human was awareness of His nothingness in Himself!

His statements about the Father often puzzled the disciples. He would say, "I do what I see the Father do," "as I hear, I judge," "My doctrine is not mine, but His that sent Me." They wondered whether He had some strange means of communication with His "Father in heaven."

He revealed their true meaning in what I think is the most important conversation ever recorded. It was the first time in actual human words that the union of man and God is revealed. It came in that last conversation at the supper table before He went out to Gethsemane.

He kept saying He was going to the Father, but the Spirit had not come; therefore, a normal human could only understand outward relationships— one person here, another there, each person separate from the other.

So when He talked about the Father, the disciples thought He must be some Being way up in the blue.

Feeling desperate that Jesus was going to whom they knew not, Philip made a commonsense request:

"Lord, show us the Father, and it sufficeth us" (John 14:8).

In other words, "Open heaven, and let us have one look at the One to whom You say You are going."

Remember Jesus' answer? He said, "Have I been so long time with you, and yet hast thou not known me, Philip? he that hath seen me hath seen the Father; and how sayest thou then, Show us the Father?" (v. 9).

Now you might stop with that statement and say, "Well, that's Deity. He meant that their names were interchangeable—Father, Son, Spirit;

and they could call Him Father or Jesus."

But He didn't mean that, for the next verse says this: "Believest thou not that I am in the Father and the Father in me? the words that I speak unto you I speak not of myself: but the Father that dwelleth in me, he doeth the works."

When He had said He did what He saw the Father doing, it was not that He had some telescopic view into heaven, but that as the Father *in* Him took Him into various situations and faced Him with various needs, He would know this was a call to action. As He saw the Father moving into action, He took action. The action of faith.

The same was true of the words He spoke. He was expressing the thoughts and words the Father thought and spoke in Him.

So you see the human nothingness and the divine union? Yet that doesn't mean that we do nothing.

No one was more active than Jesus Christ! But the activity was secondary to receptivity.

An outstanding characteristic of the life of Jesus was His relaxed attitude. He was always saying, "I have what the Father *gives* Me." Yet what words He spoke and deeds He did!

You see, that relaxed attitude is a normal human attitude—because a vessel hasn't anything except the capacity to contain. So relax!

Two, But One

Someone may say, "Well, Jesus Christ was a unique person. Can we say we're just like Jesus Christ?"

Yes, you can.

The chapter ends as Jesus says, "Arise, let us go hence." It appears to me that as they moved from the supper table toward Gethsemane, He wanted to give one other illustration to connect them up with what He had said of Himself and the Father. They passed through a vineyard.

"See," He said, "I have been the branch of my Father. He has been my vine; His sap has been flowing through Me, and I have just been bearing the fruit.

"Now," He said, "I am your vine and you are my branches. We are to have the same union which I have had with the Father, and apart from me ye can do nothing" (15:1-5, paraphrased).

Then, as a passing remark in the midst of another subject, Paul made a marvelous statement in 1 Corinthians 6:17 that reveals the nature of that union: "He that is joined to the Lord is one spirit." That's the basis for our union: one spirit.

A great many of our confusions in life begin because we haven't discerned between soul and spirit. The Bible analyzes the human personality into three parts; it speaks of "your whole spirit and soul and body" in 1 Thessalonians 5:23.

Look at the order: not body, soul and spirit—that's *our* order. God's order is spirit first: "I pray God your whole spirit and soul and body be preserved blameless."

To put it shortly, spirit is the seat of ego; soul is the seat of the emotions and of reason.

Spirit is the ego, the self. God is spirit and He is the first ego, the first self. We are spirits, of whom He is the Father (Hebrews 12:9). He is the Creator of body and soul, but the Father of spirits.

Down in that center—the spirit—is where you know and love. Knowledge and love—mind and heart—are the real self, the real person, That's where you irrevocably live.

Paul, in 1 Corinthians 2:11, said, "What man knoweth the things of a man save the spirit of man which is in him?" The knower inside us is our spirit.

For instance we Christians know Jesus Christ. How do you know Jesus Christ? I can't tell you. Somehow you've come past the realm of just knowing about this Person called Jesus Christ, and He is to you a Person.

In the same way, a person knows music, knows art, knows science.

I understand that, you say. *I'm at home with that. He knows.*

That isn't giving a reason, is it? It's

something intuitive inside him, and that's his spirit. That's different from reason.

But your soul is more external. It is how you express your spirit.

Your mind (your knowledge) *expresses* itself in reasons. But reasons can vary. They can be influenced by all sorts of things.

Your heart *expresses* itself through the affections, the emotions. That's where you feel. But feelings can vary—quite apart from the set purposes of the heart. We say, "I don't feel like this," or "I feel spiritually cold, or dead, or dry," and they are all illusions of the soul.

Neither reason nor emotion is our real life, which is deep inside us.

Now, we live where we love. That's what the Bible calls the heart. That's not the emotions; it's the set of life, the choices, the purposes where one of the two spirits is joined to us—the false spirit of self-love, called the spirit of error, who is in us from birth—or the true Spirit of self-giving, the Spirit of God, called "the Spirit of truth," who replaces the false spirit in us by redemption and rebirth.

We have to learn how to discern between soul and spirit (Hebrews 4:12). We have to refuse in our spirit, our real selves, to be dominated by the reactions of the emotions or the reasons—our souls.

When we have learned to discern and to discipline the reactions of the soul, then through our reasons and our emotions we channel Christ, and are not moved by the reflex action of the world coming back at us.

But how can I do this? you ask.

You can do this because "He that is joined unto the Lord is *one spirit,*" (1 Corinthians 6:17).

The Bible reveals that God, Who is spirit, is an invisible Person. He always expresses Himself.

He expresses the kind of Person He is through His Son, Jesus Christ.

Visible—and Invisible—Life

So with us, our spirits are our invisible selves, and we have to have a form of expression. The form of expression is the soul life.

And it's in our soul life that we differ.

In the spirit we're undifferentiated. You and I are exactly the same, eternally one person in the Spirit. You and I are the same person.

I'm sorry for you, but you've got to have me. Because we're all one!

But in our souls we differ: you're very quick and I'm slow. One person is cautious, another person is dashing. Variety is in our soul life—that is, in the emotions and the reason. These are the varied expression of the inner spirit.

Now you may say in your soul life—in your emotions or your reason, "I don't like that person."

We have an affinity with some people and not with others. We're just made like that.

But you have to move back from your soul-affections (your emotions) to the inner spirit-love.

This business of emotions is most important, because dozens of Christians live with their feet dragging with a sense of condemnation and failure because they *feel* away from God, or they *feel* cold, or they *feel* guilty, or they *feel* weak, and so on.

They haven't discerned between the variable emotions of the soul and the unvarying reality of spirit—*where God's Spirit of love is eternally our other self in our spirit.*

How can I be cold when I've got that permanent fire within me—Jesus Christ?

Move back from your soul-affections and say, "No, He's here."

How can I feel dry when I have a permanent well of water inside me—Jesus Christ?

Not Emotion, But Reality

You move back from your affections, your emotions, to the real love-center—because "He that is joined to the Lord is one spirit" (1 Corinthians 6:17).

The other verse that goes with that one, which I always think is so marvelous, is perhaps my favorite in the Bible. It is Galatians 2:20, where Paul says, "I am crucified with Christ..."

That's the old Paul out.

Then he says, "...nevertheless, I live."

That's the new Paul in Christ: a living, thinking, willing, feeling, battling human. A real person.

But listen: then he corrects himself and adds, "Yet not I, but Christ liveth in me."

He could very easily have said, "Nevertheless I live *and* Christ lives in me"—as if Christ lived near him or close by him.

But you see, he replaced self by Christ.

That's the point.

He said, "Nevertheless, I live—excuse me, the real I isn't I at all, it is Christ."

In other words, your other self is Christ.

It is not you, it's Christ.

There are two selves joined in one; and the other self is Christ.

That's why it's indivisible. That's why it's ridiculous to look around or above and try to find Christ.

You don't try to find yourself, do you? Wherever you go, you are there, aren't you?

However you feel about it, you can't escape your self.

And your other self is Christ; you can't escape Him either!

I'm sorry if Christ has to go where you go! But that's His business!

In the grace of God, Jesus Christ tied Himself to us.

Isn't that amazing? You can't escape Him.

Where you go, He goes. He's your other self; He's not you.

You're you; He's He.

You contain Him; He motivated you. And you learn the habits of this abiding life.

He is the one who lives it.

You are His means of expressing Himself.

Motivation by Jesus Christ; that's the eternal life which we who know Him have already begun!

Next we will need to examine, understand and establish how this change of relationship has taken place. How can it be when we are eternally separated from God by sin?

How can we have such a boldness, so that we can be free, happy, familiar, natural—not super-duper reverent —but ordinary, *normal* people: what God intends us to be.

4

YOUR NEW SPIRIT

I believe in a secular Christ. I do not believe in a religious Christ.

I believe one of the whole difficulties of Christianity is we've put Christ in a special building for a special occasion, with special forms of worship, special music, special everything.

Cut the special out, put your hands in your pocket, and go in your old blue jeans. Christ is a secular person.

If Christ is your other self, Christ washes dishes.

If Christ is your other self, He spanks the youngsters.

If Christ is your other self, He handles the accounting machine and runs the business.

Christ, therefore, is a very common person.

You're a very common person—I assure you that. That's why I believe in a common Christ—because He lives in common people!

Obviously, humanity has become separated from God. Before I can live in the kind of familiarity with God that He intends for me, I need to know the basis for that kind of a relationship. I need to know my title. Once I am sure of my foundations I can forget them and go ahead. Once I am sure of the road under my feet I can proceed to walk confidently.

Road to Familiarity

These are the simple facts of revelation (and we can follow their logic, as well as their tragedy and wonder):

What the Bible calls sin is in one phrase—independent self. The created self was made to contain and express the Creator Self who is selfless love.

Instead, in the person of Lucifer, probably the created being nearest to God Himself, a new and horrible form of life came into existence: a created self who refused to contain the selfless Self of God but chose to live for and by himself. Lucifer was the sin-spirit, the spirit of self-love, self-seeking and all the sins known to man that proceed from that.

The history of the creation of man in the Garden of Eden tells us what happened to our forefather. He was created to contain God in a living union, which was symbolized for him in the offer of "the tree of life in the midst of the garden."

But, as a human being with free choice, he could take another way— the way of self-love, symbolized for him in the other tree in the midst of the garden—the tree of the knowledge of good and evil.

Deceived by the lying spirit of Satan, he received into himself the spirit of error rather than the Spirit of truth, and became a child of the devil. Since then the whole human race is born with the spirit of self-centeredness in it. The Bible calls it "the spirit that now worketh in the children of disobedience" (Ephesians 2:2).

That we are all born and live under that domination is obvious, for we are all by nature egotists and self-lovers.

Anything less than God's perfection is sin, and God's perfection is perfect love. But such total love to God and our brother is totally impossible without God who is love living in us.

Two Problems Solved
What, then, has He who is Love,

and therefore must save, done to restore His lost humanity to Himself?

He has taken flesh Himself to start a new race. In the Person of His Son, Jesus, He came into history as a man called "the last Adam" (1 Corinthians 15:45), the Creator of the first. Having lived a perfect life which the first Adam failed to live, He then identified Himself totally with the fallen human race by dying for us. In that death He was so identified with us all in God's sight that the Bible says, "He hath make him to be sin for us, who knew no sin" (2 Corinthians 5:21). Thus, He died. In doing so, the Bible reveals that He effected the two supreme deliverances that were the two absolute necessities.

First, He solved God's problem (or rather, God solved His own problem) by taking upon Himself the curse of the broken law, and being made a curse for us. By the shedding of His blood, His outpoured life, He became God's "mercy seat."

By this, God could both be just and justify the ungodly, and pronounce all believers in Jesus justified from all unrighteousness—forgiven, cleansed, in His sight as if we had committed no sin; "made the righteousness of God in him" (2 Corinthians 5:21). Broken law has consequences. That is the nature of law. God, foreseeing that we should all be lawbreakers, foreordained His Son to be the "propitiation through faith in his blood" (Romans 3:25).

What God revealed to be the necessary atonement for sin, He Himself suffered. What He suffered He accepted. And His acceptance is our justification (as Romans 4:25 says, "raised again for our justification"). What is good enough for God is good enough for us. "How much more shall the blood of Christ, who through the eternal Spirit offered himself without spot to God, purge your conscience from dead works to serve the living God?" (Hebrews 9:14)

Secondly, Christ's cross and resurrection solved *our* problem. For by this means He fully effected the destruction of the old union of humanity to Satan and replaced it by the new union to Himself.

Our problem is simply that in our unredeemed life our inner self, our spirit, was united to the self-loving spirit of Satan.

As a consequence, we followed the desire of soul and body. When our bodies stimulated appetites in us, we gratified them. When our souls stirred up pride or dislike of this or hate of that or love of that—we just followed them.

We were governed by our souls and bodies.

Replacement for Soul Life

But when Christ died, "he died

unto sin once" (Romans 6:10). That means that in His death, as our Representative, our last Adam, He became separated from the sin-spirit which had invaded the human spirit—just as anybody in death is separated from his spirit. And in His resurrection, He was "quickened (made alive) by the Spirit" (1 Peter 3:18).

In other words, the Spirit of truth—God Himself—united Himself to that last Adam, and thus united Himself to all who will accept their place by faith as participators in His death and resurrection.

Here was the beginning of the new and final creation, when the usurping person was cut off from the possession he had deceitfully gained of the human spirit; when the true Owner, the living God, replaced him in all who receive Jesus.

This is no biblical theory.

This is the most tremendous and dynamic event in human history!

Here is our title to union—to permanent familiarity—with God!

This replacement will make changes in your life. For example, use this little illustration.

On Sunday morning you say your duty is to go to church. But you get a blustery day, wind and snow, and you don't feel like going. But you go.

Why? Because down inside you purpose to go. You say, "Oh, I don't feel like going, but I'm going."

There you've got the point. Now you have moved from soul to spirit, you see.

Reason is exactly the same. Reason is the faculty by which we explain things and argue about them and talk about them. Through these words I've tried to use my reason, which is my soul life, to explain what I claim to know.

I claim to know Jesus Christ. I try to explain myself to you—that's my reason.

You see, reasons can differ. That is why we can differ in our opinions and explanations—our soul life; but be one in Christ—in our spirit-life.

I've always been one to dig into things. I took up philosophy just as a hobby, and got my reason thoroughly shaken. I said to myself, "I'm really not so sure that there is a God at all. Yet," I said, "I know Him and love Him and have done so for years—yet He may not be a living Person at all!"

My reason conveyed doubts to me. My spirit said, "But I know Him!"

So do you know what I came to? I said, "Well, if God is the big illusion, I'll be a little illusion alongside Him."

You see, I would not be governed by my reason—my soul—because I had something deeper—more real.

Of course, in due time, I came out more strongly confirmed in soul, or reason, as well as spirit—knowledge. Doubts are the raw material of faith.

Have we got it clear?

The consequence of broken law which we must inevitably suffer, stated in most direct and terrible fashion again and again in the words of Jesus and the writings of the apostles, was borne by God Himself in the Person of His Son. If we ask, how can the blood of any man atone for the sin of all, the answer is that this was the blood of Deity made flesh.

The enslaved condition of humanity, through the indwelling spirit of self-centeredness, with which every man is born, was *ended* at the cross!

Christ, as our representative, died to that enslavement—that sin-spirit: and again as our representative, was raised from the dead by "the Spirit of him that raised up Jesus from the dead" (Romans 8:11).

Thus, this change of union from the spirit of self-centeredness to the spirit of self-giving becomes an actual, down-to-earth fact in the personality and experience of every human being who, recognizing and admitting his need, receives Him as Lord and Saviour.

Your old spirit is replaced by your new Spirit!

You were governed by soul and body. Now, as a redeemed person, the Spirit—His Spirit in your spirit—is master of soul and body.

You meet the demands of the bodily senses, the varying emotions of the soul stimulated by world, flesh or desire, with the affirmation of the indwelling Christ as Lord.

Soul and body becomes the manifestation of Jesus Christ.

Here, indeed, is the key to being a normal person—free, happy, familiar, natural—released from the spirit of self-love into the boundless, creative outflowing energy of the new governing Spirit that indwells you: *His Spirit.*

Here, indeed, is the key to everything.